THE BEST
DOGS
EVER

GERMAN SHEPHERDS ARE THE BEST!

Elaine Landau

LERNER PUBLICATIONS COMPANY · MINNEAPOLIS

To Rocco Staino

Lerner Publications Company
A division of Lerner Publishing Group, Inc.
241 First Avenue North
Minneapolis, MN 55401 U.S.A.

Website address: www.lernerbooks.com

Library of Congress Cataloging-in-Publication Data

Landau, Elaine.
     German shepherds are the best! / by Elaine Landau.
         p.   cm. — (The best dogs ever)
     Includes index.
     ISBN 978-1-58013-558-0 (lib. bdg. : alk. paper)
     1. German shepherd dog. I. Title.
     SF429.G37L35 2010
     636.737'6—dc22   2008030645

Manufactured in the United States of America
1 2 3 4 5 6 — BP — 15 14 13 12 11 10

TABLE OF CONTENTS

CHAPTER ONE

A TRUE FRIEND

Smart, brave, and loyal. Those are super
qualities to have. Someone who has those
qualities would make a great friend. You might
even want to meet a person like that. If so,
you're in luck! I can introduce you. You won't be
meeting a person though. You'll be meeting
a **German shepherd dog.**

A Large, Noble Dog

German shepherds are big and beautiful. Males measure about 24 to 26 inches (61 to 66 centimeters) high at the shoulder. Females are a bit smaller. They weigh between 75 and 95 pounds (34 to 43 kilograms). That's about as much as a wolf.

I bet you've seen lots of German shepherds. They are among the best-known dogs in the world. So you may think you can answer this question: what color is a German shepherd?

Are these dogs both German shepherds?

THE BEST NAME

Sometimes a pup's name really fits it. What would you call your German shepherd? Here are some ideas:

HEIDI   XENA

Diana   SARGE   Mozart

Baron

Greta   RANGER   Glory   Rex

Was your answer black and tan? Those are the most common colors. But German shepherds can be black as well. Others are sable—a deep, rich, dark brown color. There are even white German shepherds.

German shepherds can have coats with many colors.

German Shepherds can have either long- or short-haired coats. Their coats have two layers. The soft undercoat keeps them warm. Their outercoat is coarse. Rain, sleet, and snow just run off it. These dogs do well in all kinds of weather.

AN IMPORTANT POOCH

President John F. Kennedy had a German shepherd named Clipper. Clipper was not his only pet. The Kennedys also had a cat, a rabbit, hamsters, birds, and ponies. The family had other dogs too.

The Kennedy family with some of their many dogs. *Left to right:* Caroline, Jacqueline, John Jr., and John.

Heroic Hounds

German shepherds are eager, alert, and bold. They like being with their owners. These dogs will do just about anything to protect the people they love.

German shepherds have been known to perform heroic acts. They

- Wake up their owners to warn them of a fire

- Pull people from car wrecks

- Scare off robbers by barking loudly

- Pull small children away from a busy street

German shepherds are loyal to their owners.

A MOVIE STAR

Rin Tin Tin (right) was a famous German shepherd. He starred in twenty-six movies. At times, he received more than ten thousand fan letters a week.

Most German shepherd owners are very proud of their dogs. A well-trained German shepherd is fearless yet obedient. These dogs do what is asked of them. Their owners are sure they are the best dogs ever.

CHAPTER TWO

A SUPER DOG

The American Kennel Club (AKC) groups dogs by breed. Some of the AKC's groups include the sporting group, the working group, and the hound group. German shepherds are in the herding group. The dogs in this group are smart and easy to train.

A Yorkshire terrier and a German shepherd pose together. Yorkies are in the toy group and are a much smaller breed than German shepherds.

A Fabulous Farm Dog

Take a quick dog quiz. German shepherds come from:

A. France

B. Italy

C. Germany

Bet you answered C. You knew that from the dog's name. German shepherds got their start in Germany.

By the late 1800s, people in Germany used German shepherds to herd sheep. The dogs kept the sheep from straying. The dogs also protected the sheep. The German shepherd's intelligence was important. The dog had to know when the sheep were in danger. It had to sense the difference between a threat and a friend.

WHAT A WINNER!

In 1987, a German shepherd dog won Best in Show at the Westminster Kennel Club Dog Show. It was the only time in the show's history that a German shepherd ever took this honor. The winning dog was Covy-Tucker Hill's Manhattan—also known as Hatter.

Hatter was a beautiful dog. This German shepherd was also highly intelligent and great with people. Hatter won many other awards through the years as well.

Soldier Dogs

Through the years, German shepherds have been used for more than herding. During World War I (1914–1918), they worked with German soldiers to help the troops. These dogs stood guard at night. They tracked enemy soldiers.

The dogs sometimes were in dangerous situations, like this German shepherd jumping over a barbed wire fence.

German soldiers used German shepherds in World War I.

ALMOST HUMAN

One army dog trainer said this about the German shepherds he worked with:

"These animals had feelings. They hurt [and] they cried. They got sad [and] they got happy. They saved a lot of . . . lives."

At times, the dogs delivered messages to different army units. German shepherds searched for injured soldiers. German shepherds carefully dragged the wounded men to safety. The dogs also learned to spot land mines and booby traps.

Later, people brought German shepherds to the United States. German shepherds have also worked with the U.S. Army in different wars. These dogs save soldiers' lives.

U.S. Marines used German shepherds for tracking in World War II (1939–1945).

A Powerful Police Pooch

German shepherds also work with police. The dogs learn to sniff out bombs or drugs. One such dog from Utah was named Hero. Hero lived up to his name. He found more than $8 million worth of drugs.

DID YOU KNOW?

At times, police dogs have died fighting crime. Some of these brave German shepherds were given full police funerals. They were honored as a human police officer would be.

Police officers and their police dogs march in procession at a memorial service for a police dog.

Other times, German shepherds stop robbers on the run. They also find those trying to hide. Oregon police were counting on this one night after a break-in at a Kmart. The store alarm had gone off. Two officers arrived at the scene. They searched the building but found nothing. Then police brought in a trained German shepherd. The dog found the robber in minutes. He was hiding under some empty boxes at the back of the store.

Police dogs have to be ready to respond to commands at any time.

K-9 Team

This Seeing Eye dog helps his owner across the street.

GUIDE DOGS

Seeing Eye dogs help people who are blind or have trouble seeing. These dogs lead people across busy streets and other areas. German shepherds were among the first guide dogs in the United States.

A German shepherd and its trainer search for survivors at the site of the World Trade Center in New York City after the September 11, 2001, terrorist attacks.

Search and Rescue Dogs

German shepherds also search for missing people. They have found lost children, climbers, and hikers. They have found earthquake victims too. German shepherds are hard workers. People know they can depend on them. These dogs do many different jobs and do them well.

CHAPTER THREE

THE IDEAL PET—FOR SOME PEOPLE

Do you dream of owning a really great dog? Do you ever wish you had a German shepherd? Be careful what you wish for. German shepherds are terrific dogs. But they are not for everyone.

Training Your Dog

German shepherds are large, strong dogs. They must be well trained. An untrained German shepherd can be trouble. Your dog's training should begin early on. These dogs were bred to guard sheep. And your German shepherd will want to guard you. German shepherds must learn not to overprotect their owners. They cannot attack people who come near you or your family.

Basic commands like "sit" and "stay" are important for every dog to learn.

Your dog must learn to behave safely around other people. It is your job to turn your puppy into a social animal. This is all part of your dog's training.

Training a dog takes patience. It will also take lots of time. You can't play video games or go out with your friends while training your dog. So think hard before choosing a German shepherd as a pet.

Training your German shepherd takes time and patience.

You and Your Dog

You also need to spend some fun time with your German shepherd. These dogs become very attached to their owners. You will soon be the most important person in your dog's life. German shepherds don't do well when left alone. Do you plan to keep your dog in an outdoor doghouse?

If so, don't get a German shepherd.

ALL IN THE FAMILY

Don't leave your German shepherd alone in the yard. Take it on family outings. A well-trained dog can fit in at parks and picnics.

This German shepherd plays by chasing its owner's kite on the beach.

IT SHEDS ON THE BED

German shepherds shed a lot. You'll find dog fur all over the house. That means a lot of vacuuming. Make sure you are willing to help clean up after your new best friend.

German shepherds may also not do well in a tiny apartment. A puppy might seem perfect there. However, your puppy will soon be about the size of a wolf. If you live in a small apartment, a smaller dog might be a better choice.

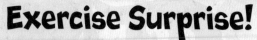

Exercise Surprise!

Are you still set on getting a German shepherd? If so, I hope you like exercise. These dogs need more than just a short walk around the block. German shepherds need real exercise. Your dog will run or jog with you. Nature hikes are another fun treat. German shepherds also enjoy playing ball and Frisbee. How about you? Do you hate exercise? If so, you might want a cat instead.

MIND GAMES

German shepherds are really smart. Exercise both their minds and bodies. Play games such as hide-and-seek with your dog.

Playing with your German shepherd and giving them lots of exercise is very important.

Of course, a German shepherd may be the perfect dog for you. You may have the time and patience to train it. Perhaps you live in a large house and love outdoor fun. If so, you have found your perfect match.

CHAPTER FOUR

WELCOME HOME

Get ready! This is the day you've dreamed of.
Your new puppy is coming home.

Are you prepared? Every dog needs some basic items. Get them before you get your dog. Here are a few things you'll need:

- collar

- leash

- tags (for identification)

- dog food

- food and water bowls

- crates (one for when your dog travels by car and one for it to rest in at home)

- treats (to be used in training)

- toys

- comb, wire brush, and shedding rake (helpful when your dog is shedding a lot)

GOOD GROOMING IS GREAT!

Brush your German shepherd daily. Give your dog a bath about four times a year. However, some dogs can get really muddy and dirty outdoors. That means more baths.

Pets and Vets—Perfect Together

A veterinarian, or vet, is a doctor who treats animals. Take your new dog to a vet right away. The vet will check your dog to be sure it is healthy. At the vet, your dog will also get the shots it needs. This is a good time to ask your vet any questions you have about your new dog.

Your dog will need more shots in the future. Take your dog for regular checkups too. And you should always take your dog to the vet if it gets sick.

Feeding Time

Your dog will need different food at different times in its life. Don't feed your dog table scraps. This can lead to weight gain and health problems. Don't give the dog too many doggie treats either.

Ask your vet about the best food for your German shepherd.

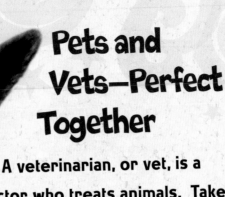

IN THE SWIM

Go swimming with your German shepherd. Let your dog get used to the water slowly. Soon you'll be playing fetch with floating toys.

Friends to the End

Be with your German shepherd as much as possible. Do things together daily. The more time you spend with your dog, the closer the two of you will become.

Your German shepherd will love and protect you. Reward your best friend's trust in you. Be the best dog owner you can be.

GLOSSARY

American Kennel Club (AKC): an organization that groups dogs by breed. The AKC also defines the characteristics of different dog breeds.

breed: a particular type of dog. Dogs of the same breed have the same body shape and general features.

canine: a dog or having to do with dogs

coat: a dog's fur

diet: the food your dog eats

herd: to keep a group of farm animals together

herding group: group of dogs that have the ability to control the movement of other animals

jog: to run at a slow, steady pace

sable: a deep, rich, brown color

Seeing Eye dogs: dogs trained to lead blind people

shed: to lose fur

straying: wandering away from a group of animals

undercoat: the soft layer of fur closest to a dog's body

veterinarian: a doctor who treats animals. Veterinarians are called vets for short.

FOR MORE INFORMATION

Books

Allen, Jean. *German Shepherds.* North Mankato, MN: Smart Apple Media, 2003. Find out more about the care and training of German shepherds.

Presnall, Judith Janda. *Police Dogs.* San Diego: KidHaven Press, 2002. Read about how dogs fight crime.

Stone, Lynn M. *German Shepherds.* Vero Beach, FL: Rourke Publishing, 2003. This book covers the German shepherd's history and characteristics.

Websites

American Kennel Club
http://www.akc.org
When you check out this website, don't miss the link Kids/Juniors. You'll find dog activity pages, dog coloring sheets, and lots of dog info just for kids.

ASPCA Animaland
http://www.aspca.org/site/PageServer?pagename=kids_pc_home
Check out this page for helpful hints on caring for a dog and other pets.

Welcome to the K-9 pages
http://www.k9man.com
Visit this website for tips on how to train your German shepherd.

Index

Photo Acknowledgments

The images in this book are used with the permission of: Backgrounds © iStockphoto.com/Julie Fisher and © iStockphoto.com/Tomasz Adamczyk; © iStockphoto.com/Michael Balderas, p. 1; © Cheryl Ertelt/Visuals Unlimited/Getty Images, p. 4; © Laszlo Willinger/SuperStock, pp. 4-5; © Alan & Sandy Carey/Photo Researchers, Inc., p. 5; © Larry Reynolds/dogpix.com, p. 6; © iStockphoto.com/Jason Lugo, p. 7 (top); © Wegner, P./Peter Arnold, Inc., pp. 7-8 (bottom); © Tracy Morgan/Dorling Kindersley/Getty Images, p. 8 (top); AP Photo, p. 8 (bottom); © Simone Mueller/The Image Bank/Getty Images, p. 9 (top); © GK Hart/Vikki Hart/The Image Bank/Getty Images, p. 9 (bottom); © Ghislain & Marie David de Lossy/Taxi/Getty Images, p. 10 (top); © Hulton Archive/Getty Images, p. 10 (bottom); © DreamPictures/Riser/Getty Images, p. 11; © iStockphoto.com/Kevin Russ, p. 12; © tbkmedia.de/Alamy, pp. 12-13; © Popperfoto/Getty Images, pp. 14, 14-15; National Archives, p. 15 (W&C 0870); © Michael C. Weimar/St. Petersburg Times/ZUMA Press, p. 16 (top); AP Photo/The Saginaw News, David A. Sommers, p. 16 (bottom); © prettyfoto/Alamy, pp. 16-17; © BIOS/Peter Arnold, Inc., pp. 17 (bottom), 28; © Andrea Booher/FEMA, p. 18 (top); © Steimer, C./Peter Arnold, Inc., p. 18 (bottom); © SuperStock, Inc./SuperStock, p. 19; © Adriano Bacchella/naturepl.com, p. 20; © Maszas/Dreamstime.com, p. 21 (top); © Fotokate/Dreamstime.com, p. 21 (bottom); © Philip Schermeister/National Geographic/Getty Images, p. 22; © iStockphoto.com/Matt Tilghman, p. 23 (top); © Jilly Wendell/Taxi/Getty Images, p. 23 (bottom); © age fotostock/SuperStock, pp. 24, 26; © iStockphoto.com/JC559, pp. 24-25; © Victoria Yee/The Image Bank/Getty Images, p. 25; © Gary D. Landsman/Flirt Collection/Photolibrary, p. 27; © Mark Raycroft/Minden Pictures, pp. 28-29 (bottom); © Mike Powell/Stone+/Getty Images, p. 29 (top).

Front Cover: © Mark Raycroft/Minden Pictures.
Back Cover: © iStockphoto.com/Eric Isselée.